responsibility
in ministry

A STATEMENT OF COMMITMENT

CANADIAN CONFERENCE OF CATHOLIC BISHOPS

Approved for publication by the CCCB Permanent Council

Art & Design:
Creative Art & Design, Publications Service, CCCB

Cover Design:
Ron Tourangeau

Photo:
Skjold Photographs p.10

Published by:
CCCB Publications
Canadian Conference of Catholic Bishops
2500 Don Reid Drive
Ottawa, Ontario
K1H 2J2
www.cccb.ca

Printed in Canada by:
Bonanza Printing

CCCB Item Number 184-318

Legal Deposit:
National Library of Canada, Ottawa
ISBN English version: 0-88997-344-X
ISBN French version: 0-88997-343-1

TABLE OF CONTENTS

RESPONSIBILITY IN MINISTRY:
A STATEMENT OF COMMITMENT

INTRODUCTION

T he CCCB Ad Hoc Committee on Responsibility in Ministry offers to the dioceses a pastoral working instrument which we hope will make a positive contribution to ministry in the Church. Most of the content and tone of the text reflect the results of an extensive consultation with more than 150 clergy, religious and lay people across the country. The parameters of the document, its application and its implementation are set out below.

1. PARAMETERS

Many official Church documents and other works examine the nature and vocation of ministry. The intent of this text is not to repeat the scriptural or theological basis for ministry but to set out briefly some of the responsibilities that are part of ministering in the Church today.

While this document is a reminder that there are professional aspects to ministry, it is not a Code of Ethics. The *Code of Canon Law*, the *Directory on the Ministry and Life of Priests*, diocesan policies and protocols, and many other official Church documents govern the rights and responsibilities of those in ministry. Most of the provisions in this document reflect ideals to inspire ministry rather than a set of rules and regulations to be enforced.

Throughout the country, countless men and women give of themselves generously in the service of God and the Christian community. Far from being a critique of current practice, the hope is that this document will deepen and renew in a personal way the commitment to serve and lead to ever more fruitful and responsible ministry.

2. APPLICATION

While all who are baptized share in the ministry and mission of Christ, not every service to others is ministry, nor need every service be officially designated as ministry to be considered worthwhile. This document is primarily addressed to those who have received an appointment or mandate from the competent authority of their diocese to minister in the name of the Church.

Including the ministries of clergy, religious, and married and single lay people in the same document underlines the fact that ministry today takes various forms and is collaborative. The application of specific provisions, however, needs to make allowances for the differences in vocation.

3. DIOCESAN IMPLEMENTATION

This working instrument should be regarded as a living document. The dioceses are encouraged to adapt it to their local situations in consultation with those concerned. The Workshop Model for Study and Reflection that accompanies this document may help in discerning what is required and desired in a particular diocese.

Members of the Ad Hoc Committee on Responsibility in Ministry

Rev. Gerry Copeman
    Chairperson of the Ad Hoc Committee, President of the
    National Federation of Councils of Priests (1992 - 1995)

Dr. Jeannine Guindon
    Psychotherapist and founder of the Institut de Formation
    Humaine Intégrale de Montréal

Sister Mary Jean Goulet, c.s.c.
    Assistant Coordinator of Pastoral Services - Faith Development,
    Archdiocese of Ottawa

Most Rev. Robert Lebel
    Bishop of Valleyfield and member of the CCCB Theology
    Commission (1991-1995)

Most Rev. Brendan O'Brien
    Bishop of Pembroke and member of the CCCB Theology
    Commission (1991-1995)

Rev. Roch Pagé
    Professor of Canon Law at St. Paul University, Ottawa

Committee Staff

Ms. Jennifer Leddy, lawyer and member of the CCCB Professional
    Pastoral Group

The committee acknowledges with gratitude the work of Joanne Chafe (Project Specialist, Adult Portfolio, National Office of Religious Education, Canadian Conference of Catholic Bishops) and Paul-André Giguère (a member of the faculty, Institut de Pastorale, Montreal), who created the resources for study and reflection that begin at page 25.

OUR COMMITMENTS

T he Pastoral Letters of St. Paul to Timothy and Titus[1] show that from earliest times, ministry was expected to be marked by love that overflows into service, stewardship, trust and exemplary personal conduct. This present document recalls these expectations within the contemporary framework of responsibility.

The call and commitment to serve God and the People of God involves accepting certain responsibilities as individuals and as members of our communities. The following commitments express to those to whom we minister, to our colleagues, to our dioceses, to the wider community and to ourselves our responsibilities as clergy, religious and lay ministers.

---

[1] See 1 Tm 4.14-16; 2 Tm 4.5; Tt 2.7-8.

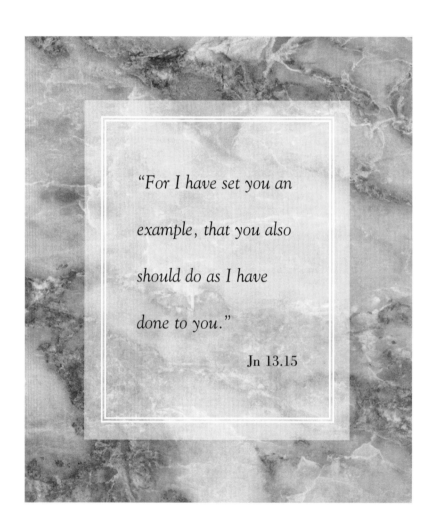

"For I have set you an example, that you also should do as I have done to you."

Jn 13.15

A. Responsibilities to Those to Whom We Minister

Desiring to minister as Jesus did and to exercise leadership that is about service, not power, and that calls and enables others to serve, we will

- strive to develop the communication and management skills that are needed in a particular milieu

- welcome regular evaluation of our ministry by colleagues and the people we serve

- acknowledge the limits of our qualifications, abilities and availability, and recommend that, where appropriate, people consult other professionals, particularly with respect to marriage and other counselling, and legal, financial, and medical matters

- try, where appropriate, to make decisions in a consultative manner and to search for consensus so that different views are heard and people respected in the process

Motivated by the desire to nourish our communities spiritually, we will

- affirm their right to well-prepared liturgical celebrations and good homilies by enhancing our knowledge of the Scriptures, Church teaching, and liturgical principles, and our public-speaking skills

- be sensitive to the diverse forms of spirituality within the Church

Desiring to be faithful stewards and to serve with justice and integrity, we will

- try to create just working conditions for employees

- create a cooperative and harmonious work atmosphere that respects family life

- exercise good stewardship of all funds and assets entrusted to our care

- avoid pressuring people to donate their professional or other skills for which they would be entitled to just remuneration

- inform ourselves of the copyright laws and respect them when using any resources, including liturgical ones

Conscious of the trust placed in us and anxious to respect and protect the dignity and integrity of all people because they are made in the image of God, we will

- maintain confidentiality and respect the privacy of people to whom we minister, unless serious harm would result

- respect the absolute confidentiality of the seal of confession

- inform ourselves of and comply with the legal obligation to report suspected child abuse

- never sexually, emotionally, or physically abuse or harass any adult, adolescent, or child

- serve each person without discrimination

- in pastoral and counselling relationships, promote the human and spiritual growth of the counsellee and respect the physical and emotional boundaries of the relationship

- not foster dependency in the people we counsel nor use them to satisfy our own needs nor take advantage of their vulnerability

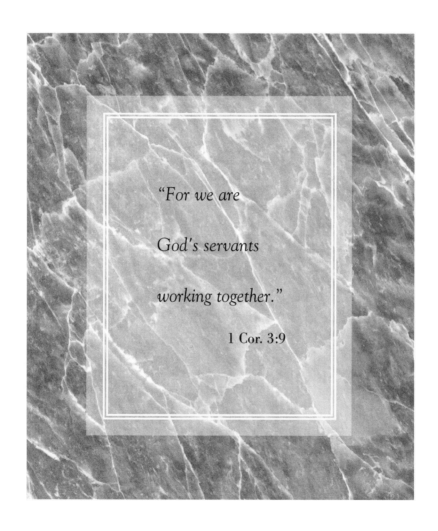

"For we are

God's servants

working together."

1 Cor. 3:9

B. Responsibilities to Colleagues

Acknowledging that many gifts are present in the Christian community and that effective ministry calls for a collaborative style, we will

- share leadership and work cooperatively with our lay and ordained colleagues, respecting their different charisms, spiritualities, qualifications, and ministries

- participate in associations of our peers, such as the deanery, council of priests, or ministry associations

- reach out with compassion and concern to colleagues who appear to be suffering or in difficulty in their ministry or personal life

Attentive to the need to respect the history of a situation, to recognize the vitality of fresh ideas, and to acknowledge that we all have different strengths and weaknesses, we will take care to

- respect the ministry of our predecessors

- refrain from interfering in the ministry of our successors

- support our colleagues' efforts to implement the teachings of the Church

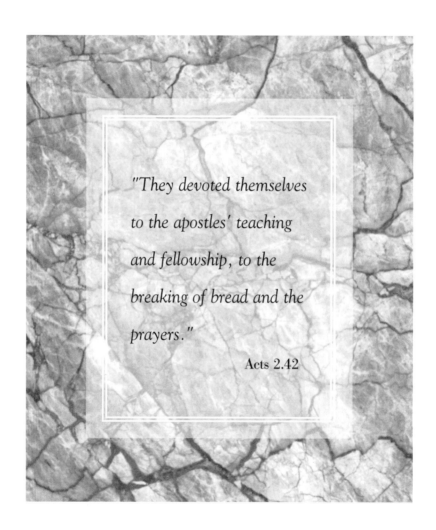

"They devoted themselves
to the apostles' teaching
and fellowship, to the
breaking of bread and the
prayers."

Acts 2.42

C. Responsibilities to the Diocesan and Universal Church

Understanding that ministry is directed to the service of God and one another, and recognizing that it is through our communion with the diocesan bishop that we affirm our unity with the Pope and the teachings of the Universal Church, we will make every effort to

- minister in communion with the diocesan bishop

- participate in the life and projects of the diocese

- follow all diocesan policies, protocols, liturgical norms, and pastoral practices

"For as the earth brings forth its shoots, and as a garden causes what is sown in it to spring up, so the Lord God will cause righteousness and praise to spring up before all the nations."

Is. 61.11

D. Responsibilities
to the Wider Community

Knowing that members of other churches are our brothers and sisters in Jesus Christ and that members of other faiths also seek to encounter God, we will endeavour to

- promote ecumenism and interfaith dialogue
- establish cooperative relationships with colleagues of other churches and faiths
- seek ways to collaborate in projects of mutual concern

Mindful that social justice is an integral dimension of the gospel, we will strive to promote

- the social teachings of the Canadian bishops and the Universal Church, particularly the preferential option for the poor
- the inherent dignity of the human person and the equality of men and women
- faithful stewardship of God's creation
- reconciliation and healing among those who feel alienated or marginalized from our Church communities

With the hope that the major social and ethical questions confronting our society will be resolved in light of the gospel and for the common good, we will

- keep informed about the major social and ethical issues of our day
- encourage the faithful to become involved
- contribute to the public debate and democratic process to the extent that we are able, without entering into partisan politics, bearing in mind our responsibility to promote communion and unity within the Christian community
- collaborate, where appropriate, with community agencies and groups and other people of goodwill

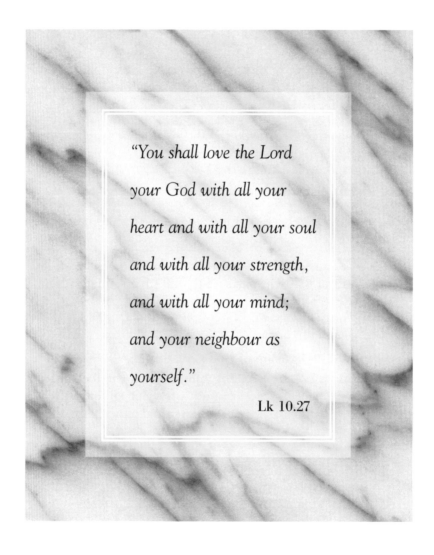

"You shall love the Lord your God with all your heart and with all your soul and with all your strength, and with all your mind; and your neighbour as yourself."

Lk 10.27

E. Responsibilities to Ourselves: Personal and Professional Development in the Service of Others

Effective ministry calls for enthusiasm and stamina; therefore, we will endeavour to care for our physical and emotional well-being through

- managing our time effectively, according to the priorities of our vocation and ministry

- developing mature friendships with men and women that are supportive of and compatible with our vocation and ministry

- acknowledging the need for adequate and private living space

- getting proper nutrition, adequate sleep, regular exercise and leisure

- avoiding substance abuse

Called to live and share our faith as fully as possible, we will strive to grow spiritually through

- daily prayer, and reflection on the Scriptures

- celebration or participation in the Eucharist and the other sacraments

- spiritual direction or accompaniment and periodic retreats

- living a simple lifestyle according to gospel values

- ongoing academic, spiritual and human formation

We embrace these commitments with the conviction that God who has called us to ministry, will sustain us by abundant grace. We rely on God's love and the support of those with whom and to whom we minister, and we take to heart the challenge to "Rekindle the gift of God that is within." (2 Tm 1.6)

RESOURCES FOR STUDY AND REFLECTION

Resources to assist with studying and reflecting on *Responsibility in Ministry: A Statement of Commitment* are included in this section. A workshop model and additional suggestions for reflection and action are provided.

WORKSHOP MODEL(S)

The workshop model is designed as a pastoral study day; however, if time is limited, it could be adapted to cover two half days (the luncheon time would delineate the break between the two half days).

If only a half day of study and reflection is available, the workshop model could be adapted. A suggested outline is provided at the end of the full workshop model.

ADDITIONAL SUGGESTIONS FOR REFLECTION AND ACTION

Suggestions in addition to the workshop model(s) are also included in this resource. These offer a variety of options for individual and group study and reflection.

RESPONSIBILITY IN MINISTRY: A STATEMENT OF COMMITMENT

WORKSHOP MODEL FOR STUDY AND REFLECTION

1. INTRODUCTION TO THE SESSION (15 min.)

- The *bishop or other leader* welcomes the participants.
- The facilitator introduces the study day by stressing the theme of professional responsibility in contemporary culture and by making links with biblical texts such as the following:

1 Tm 4.14-16

Do not neglect the gift that is in you, which was given to you through prophecy with the laying on of hands by the council of elders. Put these things into practice, devote yourself to them, so that all may see your progress. Pay close attention to yourself and to your teaching; continue in these things, for in doing this you will save both yourself and your hearers.

2 Tm 4.5

As for you, always be sober, endure suffering, do the work of an evangelist, carry out your ministry fully.

Tt 2.7-8

Show yourself in all respects a model of good works, and in your teaching show integrity, gravity, and sound speech that cannot be censured; then any opponent will be put to shame, having nothing evil to say of us.

- The facilitator then introduces the objectives, content and process for the day.

Objectives

To help participants reflect upon responsibility in ministry by

- introducing *Responsibility in Ministry: A Statement of Commitment*

- engaging in a critical, personal appropriation of the statement

- exploring possibilities for future study or action at both individual and collective levels

Content for the day

- The content for the day is the CCCB text *Responsibility in Ministry: A Statement of Commitment* and our response to this material.

Process for the day

- The day includes time to become familiar with the statement; to react to it through input, personal reflection, and group dialogue; and to discern future directions.

2. INTRODUCTION TO RESPONSIBILITY IN MINISTRY: A STATEMENT OF COMMITMENT (60 min.)

Option A

- Offer participants a handout sheet (Appendix A) on which are listed the five headings or areas of commitment covered in the statement. Invite them to jot down what they would include in a statement of commitment for their ministry in each of these areas. *(10 min.)*

- Invite participants to work on one of these areas in a small group of their choice. (Groups are made up of four persons each. If more than four persons choose an area, they may form separate groups.) Each person in the group is invited to share what he or she would put in a statement of commitment concerning the area that the group has chosen. A group recorder creates an overview of these items.

- Distribute copies of *Responsibility in Ministry: A Statement of Commitment* and Appendix B. Ask the small groups to turn to the section that covers their topic and to compare the content. Have them prepare to report to the large group on the content of the statement for their topic and describe how their own content relates to it. *(30 min.)*

  The following questions (from Appendix B) guide the discussion:
  - *What is in the document that we had already mentioned?*
  - *What is in the document that we did not mention?*
  - *What have we mentioned that is not in the document?*

- Each group reports on its section based on the questions from Appendix B, so that by the end of the reports, the plenary group has a complete overview of the Statement of Commitment. If more than one group is discussing an area, subsequent groups looking at that area could report only on any new aspects that their discussion brought to light. *(20 min.)*

Variation:

- With a group of 35 persons or less, group reporting could be done in the following manner. Participants form new small groups of between five and seven, making sure that each group contains at least one representative of each thematic area (e.g., Responsibilities to Ourselves). Each person reports on his or her area (based on the three questions in Appendix B) so that by the end of the reports, each small group has a complete overview of the Statement of Commitment. *(20 min.)*

Option B

- Offer participants copies of Appendix A, on which are listed the five headings or areas of commitment covered in the statement. Invite them to jot down what they would include in a statement of commitment for their ministry in each of these areas. *(10 min.)*

- A resource person presents an overview of *Responsibility in Ministry: A Statement of Commitment.* Distribute copies of the statement and invite participants to follow along. At each new section, the resource person invites them to comment on the ways in which the content reflects (or doesn't reflect) what they have written. *(50 min.)*

Refreshment break (15 min.)

3. CRITICAL REFLECTION ON RESPONSIBILITY IN MINISTRY: A STATEMENT OF COMMITMENT (60 min.)

- Invite participants, again in small groups, to respond to the following questions: *(40 min.)*
    - *What is most inspiring about the statement?*
    - *What are the strengths and weaknesses of the statement with respect to the needs of the diocese, including the context in which you work?*

       – *What would be helpful to add to the statement for this context or for your particular ministry?*

Distribute Appendix C. Allow 5 to 10 minutes for personal reflection before group sharing.

- Each group records its response on newsprint, then all groups post their reports. Invite participants to walk about and read the responses. Have a blank newsprint sheet accompanying each report so that those who were not in a particular group may add their comments or check off items that they particularly support. This activity could continue informally over the lunch hour. *(20 min.)*

Lunch (60 min.)

4. RESPONDING TO RESPONSIBILITY IN MINISTRY: A STATEMENT OF COMMITMENT (40 min.)

- Welcome the participants back to the session. Summarize the morning's work and introduce the work for the afternoon – to discuss personal and diocesan implications of *Responsibility in Ministry: A Statement of Commitment.*

Personal implications

- Invite each participant to reflect on how the Statement of Commitment relates to his or her own ministry. (Offer time for personal reflection.) The following questions could act as a guide: *(10 min.)*

In light of *Responsibility in Ministry: A Statement of Commitment,*

       – *What are your current strengths which are affirmed by the statement?*
       – *Which areas are most challenging for you?*
       – *Which area could potentially offer you the most growth in ministry?*
       – *Who or what could help you to grow in this area?*

Distribute Appendix D.

- After participants have had time for personal reflection, invite them to share their reflections with a neighbour in the group. *(10 min.)*

Community implications (diocese or other context)

- Invite participants to form triads (groups of three) and discuss the following question: *(15 min.)*
  - *When you think of what this Statement of Commitment could become for those in ministry in the diocese, what image comes to your mind? Why?*

Display the question on an overhead projector or repeat it aloud.

When the triads are finished their discussion, listen to a brief sampling of images and the reasons that these images were chosen.

5. FOLLOW-UP ON RESPONSIBILITY IN MINISTRY: A STATEMENT OF COMMITMENT (50 min.)

- Invite the same triad groups to brainstorm on what action could be taken to keep this document and the input from this diocesan assembly before you as a leaven or inspiration for renewal in ministry. After 10 minutes of conversation, give each group a handout sheet of additional suggestions that were raised in the consultation phase of the Statement of Commitment. (See pp. 39-40 – Additional Suggestions for Reflection and Action.) *(25 min.)*

- At the end of the discussion time, ask the group to name its recommendations or suggestions for the diocese in an open forum. These will then be referred to the appropriate structure for follow-up. *(25 min.)*

6. EVALUATION OF THE DAY (10 min.)

- Conduct an evaluation of the day (preferably in writing) and thank participants for their contribution to the dialogue.

RESPONSIBILITY IN MINISTRY:
A STATEMENT OF COMMITMENT

WORKSHOP MODEL FOR STUDY AND REFLECTION (HALF DAY)

If a half day of study and reflection is available only, the workshop model could be adapted in the following manner:

1. Introduction to the session

   - All introductory points could be made. *(10–15 min.)*

2. Introduction to Responsibility in Ministry: A Statement of Commitment

Option B

   - Shorten the overview to *30 min.*

3. Critical Reflection on Responsibility in Ministry: A Statement of Commitment

   - Offer participants Appendix C for personal reflection. *(5 min.)*
   - Invite them to share their responses with one other person (dyads). *(10 min.)*
   - Debrief the sharing in a plenary session: for example, what are their responses to the questions? *(10 min.)*

Refreshment break (15 min.)

4. Responding to Responsibility in Ministry:
   A Statement of Commitment

   Personal implications

   - Distribute Appendix D (as in the full workshop model) for personal reflection. *(10 min.)*

5. Follow-up on Responsibility in Ministry:
   A Statement of Commitment

   - Triad groups discuss how the statement could be used in the diocese (as in the full workshop model). *(20 min.)* Include discussion of the handout sheet entitled Additional Suggestions for Reflection and Action. *(25 min.)*

Appendix A

RESPONSIBILITY IN MINISTRY:
A STATEMENT OF COMMITMENT

If you were part of a team writing a common statement on Responsibility in Ministry, what would you want to include under these headings?

Responsibilities to those to whom we minister

Responsibilities to colleagues

Responsibilities to the diocesan and Universal Church

Responsibilities to the wider community

Responsibilities to ourselves

Appendix B

RESPONSIBILITY IN MINISTRY:
A STATEMENT OF COMMITMENT

What is in the document that we had already mentioned?

What is in the document that we did not mention?

What have we mentioned that is not in the document?

Appendix C

RESPONSIBILITY IN MINISTRY:
A STATEMENT OF COMMITMENT

What is most inspiring about the statement?

What are the strengths and weaknesses of the statement with respect to the needs of the diocese,
including the context in which you work?

What would be helpful to add to the statement for
this context or for your particular ministry?

Appendix D

RESPONSIBILITY IN MINISTRY:
A STATEMENT OF COMMITMENT

In light of *Responsibility in Ministry: A Statement of Commitment,*

What are your current strengths which are affirmed by the statement?

Which areas are most challenging for you?

Which area could potentially offer you the most growth in ministry?

Who or what could help you to grow in this area?

RESPONSIBILITY IN MINISTRY
A STATEMENT OF COMMITMENT
ADDITIONAL SUGGESTIONS
FOR REFLECTION AND ACTION

The following suggestions offer possibilities for reflecting and acting on *Responsibility in Ministry: A Statement of Commitment:*

- Invite all those in ministry in the diocese to a gathering at the cathedral or other suitable location. Celebrate ministry and invite participants to take part in a ritual of re-commitment and commissioning. This could be held in the evening of the study day on *Responsibility in Ministry: A Statement of Commitment.*

- Establish a diocesan committee to follow up on specific issues or ideas arising from the Diocesan Study Day on *Responsibility in Ministry: A Statement of Commitment.*

- Invite those in ministry in the diocese to a retreat or day of recollection based on *Responsibility in Ministry: A Statement of Commitment* or related to particular sections of the statement.

- Include a study of *Responsibility in Ministry: A Statement of Commitment* in seminary formation, formation for religious life, and lay ministry formation programs.

- Include a discussion of *Responsibility in Ministry: A Statement of Commitment* in spiritual direction, in annual appraisals of ministry effectiveness, and once a year on the agenda of diocesan gatherings.

- Encourage parish teams, deanery or regional grouping, Priests' Council and Diocesan Pastoral Council to include a reflection of how the Statement of Commitment is reflected in their ministry, and how the commitments could be supportive of this, at periodic meetings during the year.

- Host gatherings by specific ministries (e.g., catechists) to discuss the Statement of Commitment and to discern implications for their own ministry.

- Offer a copy of *Responsibility in Ministry: A Statement of Commitment* to all those involved in ministry in the diocese, including newcomers as they arrive, perhaps in a ritual of installation.

- Host a series of seminars on the various sections of *Responsibility in Ministry: A Statement of Commitment.* Discuss the section and identify ways and means of continuing to grow in that area of commitment.

- Set up a diocesan display on *Responsibility in Ministry: A Statement of Commitment* at the diocesan resource centre or library. The display could be an interactive one with bulletin board, posters, overhead, reports on diocesan activity and other media related to *Responsibility in Ministry.*

- Establish links on the Internet with those in ministry in other dioceses to share ideas on *Responsibility in Ministry.*

NOTES

NOTES

NOTES

NOTES

NOTES

NOTES